The Independent Director

The role and contribution of non-executive directors

D0110551

This book is part of an ongoing joint initiative by the
Institute of Directors and Ernst & Young to promote the role
and contribution of non-executive directors.

For information, contact:
Daniel Summerfield at the IoD on 020 7451 3113
Copy sales: 020 7766 8766

Price £9.95

Copyright

The publication you are reading is protected by copyright law. This means that the publisher could take you and your employer to court and claim heavy legal damages if you make unauthorised photocopies from these pages. Photocopying copyright material without permission is no different from stealing a magazine from a newsagent.

The Copyright Licensing Agency (CLA) issues licences to bring photocopying within the law. It has designed licensing services to cover all kinds of special needs in business, education and government.

If you take photocopies from books, magazines and periodicals at work your employer should be licensed with the CLA. Make sure you are protected by a photocopying licence.

The Copyright Licensing Agency
90 Tottenham Court Road
London W1P 0LP
Tel: 020 7436 5931   Fax: 020 7436 3986

Apart from any fair dealing for the purposes of research or private study, or criticism or review, as permitted under the Copyright, Designs and Patents Act, 1988, this publication may only be reproduced, stored or transmitted, in any form or by any means, with the prior permission in writing of the publishers or, in the case of reprographic reproduction, in accordance with the terms and licences issued by the CLA. Enquiries concerning the reproduction outside those terms should be sent to the publishers at the undermentioned addresses:

Director Publications Ltd
116 Pall Mall
London SW1Y 5ED

Kogan Page
120 Pentonville Road
London N1 9JN

© Director Publications 1999

British Library Cataloguing in Publication Data
A CIP record for this book is available from the British Library
ISBN 0 7494 3222 5

Printed and bound in Great Britain

Contents

3

If you want to get ahead, put the right people beside **you.**

Align yourself with 85,000 people
in over 130 countries, all of
whom are armed with the
knowledge you need to
move ahead. And stay
there. Together, we can
move forward faster.
Forward march.
www.eyuk.com

The independent director's key role

Tim Melville-Ross, former IoD director general and currently non-executive director on several company boards

The corporate governance climate in the UK over the past few years has placed the non-executive director at the forefront of media and shareholder attention. Changing practices and Stock Exchange Listing Rules have placed growing expectations on such directors to be better equipped with the requisite skills and knowledge to undertake their roles effectively.

While it is now widely accepted that non-executive directors have an important part to play in the proper running of boards, it is often very difficult to define the exact role and contribution of a non-executive director. Furthermore, the independence of these directors, both in terms of their selection to the board and also their contribution to the board's deliberations, has also become an area of concern.

As a non-executive director of several companies, I welcome this Guide which is intended to offer support and advice to both executive directors and non-executive directors of all types of companies in understanding the important role of a non-executive director in maximising the effectiveness of the board's performance.

Championing the role of independent directors in the UK

Nigel Macdonald, senior partner with Ernst & Young, and Lord Newton, professional standards director, the Institute of Directors

For a board to perform effectively, its directors must possess sufficient experience and knowledge to deal with the wide range of issues that can impinge on the company's affairs and its business environment. The board is strengthened further by the presence of non-executive directors, whose complementary skills, independent judgement and broad experience are crucial in helping the board address all its complex tasks.

This book is designed to give practical help to chairmen, executive directors and to potential and existing non-executive directors. It marks the start of the wider Independent Director initiative by Ernst & Young and the Institute of Directors, which focuses on the role, interests and needs of non-executive directors through a series of workshops, publications and events.

The book sets independent directors in the context of their potential contribution to companies' success. In addition, it examines the benefits for companies and the economy at large of developing and supporting independent directors and understanding the future challenges for them with the changing nature of business.

It's

sync

or

sink

Add
85,000
knowledgeable
people from around
the world to your team and
you'll find yourself in a powerful
position. Because when everyone moves
in the same direction, you can get to
the future first. Together, we can
speed ahead. Dive in.
www.eyuk.com

The key difference a non-executive director can make

Blamed when things go wrong, ignored when things go right, independent directors are often the most misunderstood people in business life. Henrietta Lake from The Times, looks at their role in five organisations

"The advice that is wanted is commonly unwelcome, and that which is not wanted is evidently impertinent," wrote Samuel Johnson in 1788. The non-executive director must perform a difficult balancing act, combining the roles of policeman and trusted adviser while attempting to act as an independent voice on the company board.

Ever since Sir Adrian Cadbury's committee on corporate governance reported in 1991, independent directors have been put under the spotlight and asked to demonstrate their value.

In the wake of the Cadbury reforms, they have tended to emphasise their responsibility for the checks and balances side of governance. But this should not be allowed to obscure their key task of wealth creation; they are there to drive the business forward by helping to shape policy and to ensure its long-term viability.

At times this means incurring the wrath of other board members – giving "unwelcome" or "impertinent" advice – for the greater good of the company. Sadly, much of the contribution of non-executives goes unrecognised, taking place behind the firmly closed doors of the boardroom. But it is safe to assume that when key strategic decisions are made or disputes resolved, a non-executive is involved somewhere along the line.

Bad practice

The importance of the role of a non-executive director is painfully stark at times of corporate failure. Shareholders of Sears, the ailing retail group, were forced to watch the value of the company diminish dramatically because of what was widely accepted to be the inept management and unquestioning attitude of its management and non-executive directors.

The non-executive directors were blamed for quietly presiding over the "incredible shrinking company" that led to the £548m takeover of Sears by Philip Green and the Barclay brothers. Swayed by fast-talking chief executive Liam Strong, they offered no murmur of dissent as the business gradually reduced to a pitiful state. They were held responsible for humiliating losses on disposals, redundancies and bungled restructurings – including a failure to realise value from the Selfridges demerger. Several of the non-executives resigned in disgrace after the fiasco.

Good practice

Fortunately, the role of non-executive directors in challenging the effectiveness of the directors and arbitrating in boardroom struggles is often more positive. When Fisons – one of the

brightest stars in the pharmaceuticals industry in the 1980s –
fell from grace, shareholders and the non-executive directors
played an instrumental part in helping the then chairman,
Patrick Egan, stabilise the company and bring it under the
helm of a competent chief.

Problems began in 1991, when Fisons was first seen to have
run foul of the US Food and Drug Administration (FDA). US
sales of its Opticrom anti-allergic eyewash were hit. Things took
an ugly turn when the FDA not only revealed that the company
had been keeping its pharmaceuticals in beer kegs but that it had
admitted to bribing doctors to prescribe its asthma drug, Tilade,
and to offering discounts to distributors to inflate sales returns.

The crises led to the departure, in 1992, of John Kerridge, who
had combined the role of chairman and chief executive. On
his departure, the roles were split, but the new chief executive,
Cedric Scroggs, was ousted by Egan and his non-executive
directors when the instruments division, for which he had
particular responsibility, plunged into loss. Egan brought in
the group's third chief executive in three years, Bowater's
Stuart Wallis – a man with a reputation for turning around
problem businesses. After a period of savage restructuring,
Wallis restored Fisons' fortunes. It was later sold to Rhône-
Poulenc, the French chemicals giant, for £1.8bn.

Role in corporate governance

Sir Alick Rankin and Anglo-American have recently provided
a good example of the role of the non-executive director in
corporate governance. The former chief executive of Scottish
and Newcastle Breweries played a key part in the London
flotation of the South African mining giant this year.

In April, Rankin became deputy chairman of Anglo, heading a string of heavyweight non-executive directors and charged with enabling the group to meet UK corporate governance standards in preparation for a listing on the FTSE 100. Anglo was already in the midst of a massive restructuring, unburdening itself of non-core assets. It was, however, being criticised for its complex financial structure and lack of accountability.

The City wanted a smaller and more transparent board structure, the elimination of minority shareholdings and a demonstrable commitment to the UK. There were also worries about the fact that Anglo was relying on a code of ethics that did not meet compliance rules and needed updating in the area of human rights and the environment.

Sir Alick and his non-executives were entrusted with a weighty task, and their work is by no means at an end: following the listing in June 1999, the mining giant wants to keep faith with its investors. The fact that they were given the job, however, shows how great the responsibilities of non-executives can be.

Of course, a fully rounded non-executive director is not only capable of challenging the executive directors on their stewardship and of smartening corporate governance practice but also of providing fresh ideas and a different perspective on activities. In a business environment buzzing with mergers, rationalisations and globalisations, successful companies are constantly having to operate on new frontiers. An independent person is often best placed to ask the right questions: what, for example, are this company's contingency plans for the millennium bug; how will it be affected if Britain joins the euro?

In merger talks where the tables are turning and the price no longer appears so attractive, or in boardroom discussions where the directors are keen to press ahead with an investment or divestment, non-executives can provide the "reality check".

Role in business growth

Some of the strategic aspects of the non-executive director's role are most obvious at small companies, where the objective is business growth. Adding an experienced and independent voice to the board can mean the difference between abortive and successful expansion.

When James Sommerville and Simon Needham, founders of design consultancy The Attik, wanted to expand they brought in two non-executive directors. David Addenbrook, a retired steel industry executive and Richard Cooper, an accountant, made up for the founders' lack of accounting skills. The latter also offered advice on special projects, such as the publication of their book, *Noise*.

Sommerville and Needham say they appreciated the perspective non-creatives brought to the business. Their move certainly seems to have worked. The Attik has become a 150-strong, £15m-concern with offices in New York, San Francisco and Sydney and can name Channel 4, MTV, Nike and Virgin Atlantic among its clients. This could not have been achieved, say the partners, without their non-executives. The consultancy has also employed non-executives in its US and Australian offices.

Another prime example of an organisation that is putting its independent directors to good use is Shakespeare's Globe theatre in London. Peter Kyle, general director, believes that he would be foolish not to take full advantage of the expertise of outsiders, who have provided essential advice on everything from foreign markets to fund-raising and acted as a sounding board for ideas. He says the key is to give the non-executive director a defined role so as not to create "floaters".

Sir Oliver Wright, former ambassador to Washington in the 1980s, offered his specialist knowledge when the Globe set up several "centres" in the United States to provide educational activities and raise funds (tax laws in the US are more conducive to donations by individuals than they are in the UK). Sir Oliver provided valuable introductions and came to the rescue when one of the US centres was feeling isolated from the rest of the company.

The Globe's non-executives and board of trustees have an essential function as ambassadors and networkers for the theatre in its fund-raising activities. Unusually for an arts centre, the Globe set out to be self-financing and must rely for almost all its funding on the private sector. Private and corporate donations and sponsorship have already paid for the £24m-worth of building on the site, but more money is needed to complete the ambitious project.

The Globe's experiences point to the non-executive's role as credibility provider. Having a "name" on the board can certainly help raise capital. When the Globe needed to approach a bank to raise funds in a short space of time it received invaluable help from one non-executive in particular – Sir Evelyn Rothschild.

Functions of the board

To understand the purpose of a non-executive director one has to first understand the purpose of a board. Lord Newton, the IoD's professional standards director, defines the board's key responsibilities

The role of the non-executive director, be it in a large multi-national or a small growing enterprise, is complex. At its most general, it involves bringing experience and expertise to all the work of the board. Much more specifically, the role involves playing a key part in helping ensure that the company is kept under control, both indirectly by the shareholders and directly by the board. It must necessarily be seen in the context of the wide duties and responsibilities of the board of directors itself.

This chapter focuses on those duties and responsibilities. It is based on the IoD's report, *Standards for the Board*, the leading reference guide on good practice for boards of directors.

Challenges for the board

Standards for the Board states that the board's key purpose "is to ensure the company's prosperity by collectively directing the company's affairs, whilst meeting the appropriate interests of its shareholders and relevant stakeholders". It is for the board to judge, on a case-by-case basis, which stakeholders it treats as "relevant" and which of their interests it is appropriate to meet, taking into account the law, relevant regulations and commercial considerations. In pursuing this key purpose, a board of directors faces a uniquely demanding set of responsibilities and challenges. It also faces a range of objectives that can sometimes seem contradictory. The board:

▶ must simultaneously be entrepreneurial and drive the business forward while keeping it under prudent control;

▶ is required to be sufficiently knowledgeable about the workings of the company to be answerable for its actions, yet able to stand back from the day-to-day management of the company and retain an objective, longer-term view;

▶ must be sensitive to the pressures of short-term issues and yet take account of broader, long-term trends;

▶ must be knowledgeable about "local" issues and yet be aware of potential or actual wider competitive influences;

▶ is expected to be focused on the commercial needs of its business while acting responsibly towards its employees, business partners and society as a whole.

Each board member is expected to recognise these challenges and ensure that they personally contribute to finding the right balance between these various competing pressures. In seeking to do so, executive directors may find it difficult to see beyond their direct focus on the business and its day-to-day problems; non-executive directors, on the other hand, may find it difficult to feel sufficiently informed about the direct day-to-day pressures faced by the company.

Tasks of the board

It is, of course, impossible to list every task that each individual board of directors has to carry out. Each board has to consider its own situation and circumstances. For example, small privately owned companies might not be concerned with many of the issues that preoccupy large listed companies.

However, *Standards for the Board* does attempt to highlight the broad tasks that are pertinent to every board and also the indicators of good practice that can help boards of directors reflect on how they are fulfilling those tasks. Hence, it is argued, boards can be helped greatly by focusing on four key areas:

▶ establishing vision, mission and values;

▶ setting strategy and structure;

▶ delegating to management;

▶ exercising accountability to shareholders and being responsible to relevant stakeholders.

Each of these can be broken down into separate elements (as seen in the checklist box at the end of this chapter).

Each board should decide what it needs to do in order to achieve its overall purpose and identify any gaps or deficiencies in what it is already doing. The board is also encouraged to focus on those tasks that it must – or wishes to – undertake itself and to decide which should more properly be carried out by senior management. Many boards of larger companies devise a schedule of reserved powers that explicitly distinguishes between those tasks that are to be the sole responsibility of the board and those that can legitimately be devolved to senior managers.

The effective board

Within a company, the board of directors is the principal agent of risk taking and enterprise, the principal maker of commercial and other judgments. Discharging these responsibilities means thinking not only about particular tasks but also about ways of working as a board, and ensuring individual directors can be fully equipped to play their part. Again, there are four particular areas worthy of time and energy:

▶ determining board composition and organisation;

▶ clarifying board and management responsibilities;

▶ planning and managing board and board committee meetings;

▶ developing the effectiveness of the board.

These activities are normally undertaken by the chairman of the board, part of whose role is to manage the board's business and act as its facilitator and guide.

Where the managing director is also the chairman, it is important that these two distinct roles are properly separated and that sufficient attention is given to carrying out the chairman's role effectively. The board should not be just an executive team.

The non-executive directors play an important part in assisting the chairman to fulfil his role by regularly and rigorously assessing the effectiveness of the board's processes and activities. Given their outside perspective, they are sometimes best placed to ensure that the board focuses its energies effectively on meeting the demands described earlier.

The context for the non-executive director

Each board of directors is faced with unique problems and circumstances that must be addressed for the company to be truly successful. As this chapter has sought to show, however, there are some universal challenges that are faced by all boards and a number of strategic tasks that any board must perform if its central purpose is to be achieved.

Legally speaking, there is no distinction between an executive and non-executive director. UK company law does not see the roles as distinct and therefore does not distinguish between their responsibilities. Yet there is inescapably a sense in which the non-executive director's role can be seen as balancing that of the executive director, so as to ensure the board as a whole functions effectively.

Where the executive director has an intimate knowledge of the company, the non-executive director may be expected to have a wider perspective of the world at large. Where the executive director may be better equipped to provide an entrepreneurial spur to the company, the non-executive director may have more to say about ensuring prudent control.

At the end of the day, however, it is important to be clear that the challenges and tasks discussed in this chapter are those of the board, not of individual directors. While each individual may have a distinct contribution to make, it is the collective responsibility of the board to ensure the company's successful operation. The non-executive director's particular contribution is the focus of other chapters in this guide.

An overview of the tasks of the board and indicators of good practice

A. Establish vision, mission and values

A.1 Determine the company's vision and mission to guide and set the pace for its current operations and future development.

A.2 Determine the values to be promoted throughout the company.

A.3 Determine and review company goals.

A.4 Determine company policies.

B. Set strategy and structure

B.1 Review and evaluate present and future opportunities, threats and risks in the external environment; and current and future strengths, weaknesses and risks relating to the company.

B.2 Determine strategic options, select those to be pursued, and decide the means to implement and support them.

B.3 Determine the business strategies and plans that underpin the corporate strategy.

B.4 Ensure that the company's organisational structure and capability are appropriate for implementing the chosen strategies.

C. Delegate to management

C.1 Delegate authority to management, and monitor and evaluate the implementation of policies, strategies and business plans.

C.2 Determine monitoring criteria to be used by the board.

C.3 Ensure that internal controls are effective.

C.4 Communicate with senior management.

D. Exercise accountability to shareholders and be responsible to relevant stakeholders

D.1 Ensure that communications both to and from shareholders and relevant stakeholders are effective.

D.2 Understand and take into account the interests of shareholders and relevant stakeholders.

D.3 Monitor relations with shareholders and relevant stakeholders by the gathering and evaluation of appropriate information.

D.4 Promote the goodwill and support of shareholders and relevant stakeholders.

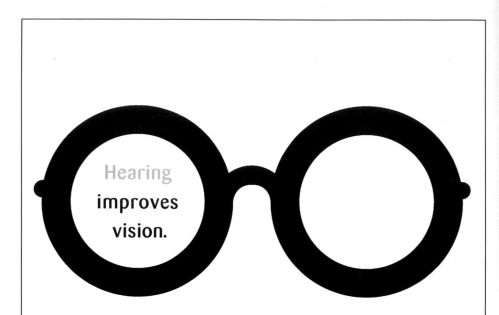

Hearing improves vision.

Solutions that are individually designed to fit your growing needs can only come from people who listen better. And see farther. Together, we can think bigger and achieve more. Let's talk.

www.eyuk.com

What is an independent director?

Every year, Patrick Dunne, a director of 3i, one of Europe's leading venture capital companies, helps hundreds of companies find non-executive directors. Here, he outlines the process that companies should adopt when deciding they need a non-executive director

Adding someone to the board is a deeply personal thing for any company whether it be a FTSE100 company or a business start-up. Any change, executive or non-executive, affects the team dynamic. So it is important to get it right.

At 3i, we have long believed in the power of good independent directors to add value to our investments. This is why we have developed an international programme of more than 500 members. We now make several hundred independent chairman or director appointments a year. For any individual appointment to work the starting point must be to consider: "What is it we are looking for and why?"

Clarity in this makes it a lot easier to find appropriate people. Confusion as to why you want to add, change, or perhaps even recruit your first non-executive director will result in success only with a great deal of luck.

Apart from the specifics relating to your business, are there any general characteristics to look out for in an independent director? Before we can answer this we need to think about the job of the board. There are three generic things a board does no matter what the size, location or sector of the enterprise. These are to do with "the right strategy", "the right resources" and "keeping out of jail".

The job of the board is to ensure that the right strategy is in place, that it is being implemented and that it is regularly reviewed. The board also needs to ensure that the right resources are available – by far the most important being people and money. "Keeping out of jail" simply means that the business needs to comply with all the regulations and agreements relevant to its particular circumstances.

The independent director's role

So what is the independent director's role in this? Crucially, it is to help the executive directors achieve their business objectives – though you could be forgiven for thinking otherwise from reading the press or much of the literature on the subject.

Most of what is written is to do with policing and governance. Important though these aspects are, they are only part of the role. If your board meetings are just a show for the non-executive directors or seen as a "good morning's sport in trying to catch the executive out" then you'll get what you deserve: a bunch of "board pack" directors, with whom you have little empathy.

If you can approach finding an independent director with a positive frame of mind rather than thinking of recruiting someone who is there to slow you down, to check up on you, to be an adornment or to appease others, you are far more likely to get a good match. A focus on finding someone who will help you with decisions about strategy and resources as well as someone who has the experience to ensure that appropriate corporate governance is in place will be well worthwhile.

Thinking about your board as a team and the independent director as a member of that team is another important context. You need a fit in terms of complementary skills, experience and personality. One of the most important things from our perspective is for the management teams to pick someone they believe will be useful to them.

So what general qualities do we and they look out for? Probably the most underused word in business is "judgment". One of the defining characteristics of an excellent independent director is good judgment of people and commercial situations. However, a fine sense of judgment won't be enough on its own. The "irritatingly right" are no use at all if they can't get heard. So the ability to "influence" needs to be added to the list of defining qualities.

How do these two qualities, judgment and the ability to influence, manifest themselves and why are they so relevant? Let's start with judgment. It's vital because most boards will only have four or five really significant things to decide each year. An independent director who can help you decide what these things are and then be able to provide valuable insights into each of them is therefore key.

One of my favourite business cartoons is of a non-executive turning to the finance director and saying: "The addition is correct but where is the money?" In order to maintain a fine sense of judgment, close contact with reality is required.

'Real world calibration'

Keeping a grip on the real world is tricky for highly successful executives. Dangerous feelings of invincibility and occasional delusions of competence may emerge unless someone gives you a regular dose of real world calibration. An independent director you respect and who also has broad and current experience of other businesses should be able to fulfil this role.

At 3i, we have found that those who have led successful entrepreneurial ventures – be they start-ups or buy-outs or buy-ins – are particularly useful. A sense of ownership seems to sharpen acumen. However, be careful not to get someone who is too rampantly entrepreneurial. The "control freak" tendency may be just too strong!

Since internationalisation is an important component of strategy for most businesses today, it might be useful to pick someone who has experience of operating in other countries. This is also important for other reasons: we have found that those who have spent time overseas have often developed a stronger resilience, independence of mind and tolerance of alternative viewpoints.

Interviewing candidates

So how do you tell whether someone has good judgment from an interview? Track record clearly provides an indication, but the first signal you get when you meet them is that they will find it hard to get in the door because of the size of their ears: they are great listeners and are unlikely to drone on about the people they know or famous past victories.

They will behave like good independent directors in the interview, listening carefully and asking short but thought-provoking questions. They will try to get a good feel for your strategy for the business and the ownership. By talking through current issues you should also get a feel for their influencing style and whether they can be trusted.

Bear in mind that it is hard to influence people who don't respect you — no matter how user-friendly you are. An impressive track record may help generate respect, but real respect comes through the combination of achievement and personality.

What sort of personality should you be looking for? Good listening skills have been mentioned earlier. Two other vital attributes are vigour and rigour. Gaining proper familiarity with a business and becoming a valued member of the board team requires considerable commitment. In order to be of real use in discussing complex issues, a rigorous mind and one that is good at absorbing information is also required.

A "cuddle and kick" personality is needed. You must find someone who will provide both encouragement as well as ensuring that there is appropriate corporate governance. Confident humility and calm wisdom are traits of the natural confidant. You should feel able to confide in your independent director and he or she should have the confidence to debate the things closest to your business heart. It may also be worth considering why he or she is prepared to join your board and what the motivation is. The best reasons are seldom financial. This is not to say they won't want to be fairly rewarded – just that interest in your business and a passion for the business world are vitally important.

One final characteristic of a good independent director is recognising when it is time to go. Perhaps this is the ultimate proof of good judgment.

A characteristic of those who succeed in picking really effective independent directors is that they research their candidates with skill and care. They make sure they talk to other managing directors who have them on their boards.

"You could really do with a decent non-executive director." This often well-intended remark is received in a variety of ways. Many hear it as implied criticism, others – usually those doing well – fail to see its relevance. The wise listen and, if it is right, turn it into an opportunity.

Patrick Dunne is responsible for the independent directors programme as well as group marketing at 3i, which is Europe's leading venture capital company. He is a regular boardroom commentator and author of Running Board Meetings *and* Directors Dilemmas, *published by Kogan Page, and is a visiting fellow at Cranfield School of Management.*

The meaning of independence

Conflict of interest corrupts. Nigel Macdonald, senior partner with Ernst & Young, explains the importance of independence to the non-executive role

The role of the independent director is seen surprisingly differently on different boards. Even "official" guidelines on the role can vary significantly – in emphasis if not in substance.

The 1998 Hampel Report notes approvingly that "non-executive directors are normally appointed to the board primarily for their contribution to the development of the company's strategy."[1] The Cadbury Committee's 1992 report also says that non-executive directors should bring an independent judgment to bear on questions of strategy, but additionally believes they have a role to play in performance, standards of conduct and the management of resources – including key appointments.

The OECD casts the net further still. Its *Principles of Corporate Governance* paper looks to the non-executive director to do those things Cadbury and Hampel identify but also, and explicitly, to achieve a balance by "monitoring and managing potential conflicts of interest of management, board members and shareholders."[2] Thus "boards should consider assigning a sufficient number of non-executive board members capable of exercising independent judgment to tasks where there is a potential for conflict of interest."[3]

Despite these differences, several common themes apply to the role of independent director. These may be grouped under the headings of direction, monitoring and balance.

Direction

The independent director should be able to guide the direction of the company, both in contributing to and influencing the development of strategy, and in helping to select and monitor the executive team needed to implement that strategy.

If we accept that it is people and their skills that matter over and above processes or industrial positioning, then picking the right management team becomes the most important decision a board can make. The difference between good and adequate management is that the former will turn a difficult situation to advantage, while the latter can allow a good situation to deteriorate through lack of drive or entrepreneurial talent. Strategic planning is, of course, essential, but good team building must come first.

Monitoring

Clearly, monitoring is an integral part of direction. You cannot help steer a company if you do not keep a check on what is going on. The independent director is ideally placed to assume the monitoring role because he or she is not wound up in the day-to-day running of the company. If you are the executive whose job it is to implement the strategy, it is hard to monitor yourself. A separation of powers is necessary; appointing independent directors can achieve it.

The monitoring role, however, is not exclusive to strategic direction. It relates also to the legal obligations of directors and to their responsibilities to shareholders. The independent director must ensure that the company has appropriate financial controls and that they are working, and that the company addresses the risks of the business. The latter is a responsibility highlighted in the Stock Exchange's Combined Code and is amplified in the section on Business Risk Management in the 1999 Turnbull guidelines.

It should, of course, be remembered that there is no such thing as a risk-free commercial environment. In a profitable business, the skill lies in achieving the right balance between procedural disciplines and entrepreneurial activity. Too much control not only costs too much but also leads to paralysis of business initiative. The independent director who is constitutionally risk-averse can hold the company back.

Another, and very specific, area of monitoring is the remuneration of directors. Independents often make decisions on executive pay in remuneration sub-committees.

Balance

An area of potential conflict, which is brought out very strongly in the OECD guidelines, occurs in situations when the stakeholders have diverging interests. The independent directors have a particular responsibility to ensure that at those times the management interests do not dominate. Where remuneration incentives are well chosen, management interests can be aligned quite closely to those of the shareholders. However, the interests of other stakeholders, such as customers, employees and members of the community must also be kept in mind. It is widely accepted that a company that cares little for this broader group of stakeholders is unlikely to succeed for long.

Takeovers can call for the most delicate of balancing acts, leading to fundamental tensions between management and shareholders. When a hostile bid is made, management may fear, or even know, that their own jobs will be at risk. There are many examples where it appears that management would have fought to the death to prevent a takeover, even though the price offered looks to have been in the shareholders' best interests.

True independence

In addition to these questions of responsibilities there is a broader issue that is both practical and philosophical. This revolves around how we identify and encourage independence. In short: what does "independence" mean? It is easier to state at the outset what it does not mean: the independent director should not come as the puppet of a certain group of managers or shareholders.

Nor should he or she be appointed purely because he or she is a golfing chum of the chairman. On the contrary, independent directors should be strong in their ability to think the unthinkable and to stand up for what they think is right.

There is a distinction to be made between the two terms "non-executive" director and "independent" director. Put simply, all independent directors are non-executives but not all non-executive directors are independent.

In a situation where, let us say, a company has acquired a 25 per cent stake in another, it is not unusual for the latter to offer its new major shareholder a non-executive directorship on its board. Indeed, there are perfectly valid reasons to do so. But the person so appointed is normally there specifically to look after the interests of a particular group of shareholders – he is not truly "independent", so long as the minority shareholding can be disposed of separately.

Non-executive directors who are truly independent are appointed precisely because they are not a potential hostage to any one interest group or faction within the organisation or among its other stakeholders.

Remuneration

It follows that the remuneration of non-executive directors is an issue. Historically, there have been examples of non-executive chairmen being paid much more than many executive directors in the same company.

Naturally, independent directors need to be paid for their services; but the figure should not be so high as to raise questions about their financial independence from the company in which they serve. Indeed, true independence arises when the independent director is capable of exercising the ultimate sanction of walking out.

A related question is whether non-executive directors should be allowed to have share options. If they are, their rewards are more aligned with those of the shareholders, but the options may have the effect of locking them into the company.

Just as important as financial independence – and it could be argued, the quintessence of a good non-executive director – is independence of mind.

A key business skill is the ability to spot the opportunity created by a new way of doing things and the threat presented to the company if someone outside it does that "new thing" first. Many directors fail to recognise that relying on precedent can frustrate progress. The way that "we've always done" something is not necessarily the right way. It is only an assumption that all have accepted. Recognising that and rethinking the assumption can, on occasion, lead to a breakthrough from which real commercial advantage can be gained.

Independent-minded people will ask whether there are alternative ways of achieving the company's set goals. It should be possible for the independent director to challenge, for example, whether a project is better implemented by using existing skills, by hiring new personnel, by partnering or by acquisition.

Access to information

The independent director needs to be in a position to articulate not only where alternative methodologies may assist the attainment of corporate objectives, but also where something is actively going wrong in the management process. This means that he or she needs free access to information. As Cadbury puts it: "Non-executive directors lack the inside knowledge of the company of the executive directors, but have the same right to access to information as they do. Their effectiveness turns to a considerable extent on the quality of the information which they receive and on the use which they make of it."[4]

It is all too easy for executives, either by accident or design, to ration the availability of strategic information. They must not be allowed to do so.

Constructive challenge

Does this mean that there is often conflict between executive directors and independent directors? On an ideal board, the answer is no; the roles should be complementary. The glue that holds all directors together, whether executives or otherwise, is the common objective of driving the company forward, in the interests of the shareholders. The independent director does this by challenging constructively the key assumptions made by executive colleagues. No person is uniquely right, and it is through constructive challenge that performance is improved, both at the personal and the corporate level. In a good board, the tension this creates is creative.

So, to summarise, the true independent director requires a varied (and valuable) set of skills. He or she needs the ability to challenge without personal attack, to judge people as well as issues, to assess risk but not be frightened by it, to have the force of personality to influence executive management and to do all this from a position of impartiality and autonomy. Finding and retaining such people is no mean task. But this in itself underscores the importance of the independent director to business – both now and in the future.

1. Hampel Report, 3.8

2. OECD Principles of Corporate Governance, V.D.4

3. OECD Principles of Corporate Governance, V.E.1

4. Cadbury Report, 4.14

Recruitment and selection

Honesty, knowledge, experience, courage, vision, diplomacy...the list of desired attributes for a non-executive director is long. But, says the Hon. Barbara Thomas, chairman of Whitworth Group, eagerness to please is not on it

Board directors often used to be cronies or chums of the chairman, not much more than ego massagers for him and the chief executive. In the past few years, however, there has been a realisation that boards have a real role to perform and that more professionalism is needed at the boardroom table.

The UK is increasingly adopting the principle of separating the roles of chairman and chief executive. The non-executive board tends to be responsible to the chairman, while the executive directors tend to be responsible to the chief executive. This means that an important check and balance has developed.

The nominations committee, which is technically made up of non-executives, has become much more important in the selection of directors. This, again, helps ensure that you do not have friends of the management filling up the board. Executive recruitment firms are increasingly being called on to find non-executive directors. Several executive recruiters specialise in locating good candidates for non-executive appointments and they do a good job in gathering CVs and in helping compile a shortlist to submit to the nominations committee.

This is not to say that people known to the chairman or chief executive should not be considered; merely that there should be a control on selection. Candidates should be interviewed thoroughly by people on the nominations committee who do not know them as well as the people putting them forward. The point is that the process is more sound if it is not a one-horse race. There should be a genuine choice.

Adding value

The changing role of the non-executive director makes getting the right people even more important. The sole purpose of the non-executive is not to sit on the board committees – nomination, audit or remuneration. That is part of their duties but it is not the only reason for them to be there.

Lots of people in this country are professionally qualified to sit on board committees. A good non-executive director must do more than that – he or she should add value to the business, and that is a more difficult quality to find.

Whether or not a non-executive director comes from the same industry as yours, you want him or her to help fill "gaps". If the company is weak in marketing, you might look for a candidate with a marketing background; if the company is worried about its financial controls, you might want someone from an audit background.

Diversity is crucial on the board. You ought not to have three non-executive directors from a financial services background, for example – even if the company is in financial services. You need people from different industries to bring a different perspective.

It is also a good idea to have an international director, or a director with international experience. This is important even for a company that is currently based in the domestic market. Everyone is thinking about having a global business these days. You don't have to fly someone over from the US or Singapore, but it's helpful to have people on the board who have experience of other countries.

City connections are often cited as a key asset for a non-executive director. They are certainly important, especially for a non-financial services company. Whether you are a manufacturing company or a technology company, a media or leisure company, you will have to deal with the City if you want to raise money. If you do not have any executives with City experience or connections this could prove difficult. A good way for non-executives to increase shareholder value (which is their primary purpose) is to help build the relationship with the City.

Good connections in general are important. The board can be seen as part of the "outreach" function of the company; part of the way a company that does one thing really well can become more involved in the world in which it lives.

People on the board are to some degree a role model for the employees in the company. This is another reason to take the composition of your board seriously. For example, having a woman or two on the board can act as an incentive to female employees. It sends a good signal to your personnel that there is a future higher up.

The boardroom mix

Should all non-executive directors be – or have been – executives on other boards? Experience is certainly important. In the UK we retire people early; someone who has been a chief executive and is just stepping down would be a very good non-executive, having good experience and contacts. I believe it is important to have had a real business career.

Above all, however, what you need are people who are strategic and visionary and can make things happen. This means that it is usually a mistake to have more than one accountant on your board. This is not to ignore the huge value of numeracy; merely to suggest that accountancy is not the sole preparation for a business career. Fortunately, the pool of obvious candidates today is wider: MBA degrees and business schools have seen to that.

But how do you tell whether someone has this visionary quality? If you are a small company that cannot afford to pay specialist headhunters for recommendations, it may be a question of word of mouth. You can certainly check out a candidate and how they are thought of through the boards they sit on – you can do it yourself if you are a chairman.

People will usually give you enough details on which to make a judgment. Chairmen who spend their lives talking to other people will know where to get good advice. Call a competitor; call someone in a related field. Do not, however, reject the idea of expensive headhunters out of hand. They are often good value for money in the long run.

Thankfully, the number of objective yardsticks for judging merit is increasing. The IoD's new Chartered Director qualification will be particularly useful in assessing younger candidates for non-executive directorships. It is a way to determine whether a person has the knowledge and experience you need. It provides younger people with a tool to make valuable contributions to the board.

Meeting the candidates

The interviewing process is really important. It is where you find out if a candidate will fit with the chemistry of the board, with its values and culture. Remember though, you cannot and should not be one happy family; you want people who will ask the hard questions.

One of the most important things for a non-executive director, however, is to be tactful and diplomatic – if you have those qualities you can say things that people do not always want to hear. The key is to be independent, know your own mind and have a reputation for being straightforward and thoughtful as well as not being afraid to speak up; to view your role as a challenger, to put up the straw man, to think of the other way, to force the board to think out of the box. To do that, you need to have had a measure of success in your own career; otherwise, people will not respect your judgment.

It may mean that other board members may think of you as formidable or tough. But that's not all bad. Remember, the role of the non-executive director is to be challenging and helpful – not to be just a "yes" man.

From the company's point of view, the interview is supremely important. Remember, however, that this is not be the time for any esoteric techniques. It's hard for a candidate to be interviewed by three or four people at one time. As soon as you put three people in a room everybody starts to posture. You only really understand somebody if you have a one-to-one conversation. You want to be able to look them in the eye and try to determine whether they are a straightforward person. That is almost impossible to do if you are talking to two people at the same time.

Today, more and more people want to be non-executive directors. There are few signs that the pool of available talent is shrinking because of directors' increased liabilities; the trick is to pick the right person. Remuneration, however, should reflect legal liability. People need to understand that this is a serious job and be paid accordingly.

The non-executive's most important contribution is made when the company is in trouble. Non-executive directors really come into their own in a crisis and that's when they work very hard. Therefore, you need people who are good at crisis management, good at thinking quickly on their feet and good at being very strategic. It is important when choosing a non-executive to think about that time in the life of a company.

Recent examples have shown that non-executives are wielding greater power in their most important role – that of ousting the chairman or chief executive if necessary. This underlines the point about true independence. Ultimately, non-executive directors are responsible to the shareholders. Their job is to increase shareholder value. Those concerned about shareholders have to look at management with a critical eye.

So where are we? The world of non-executive directors is evolving as we speak. If you choose a good one you will have an invaluable resource – so work hard at the choice – its worth it.

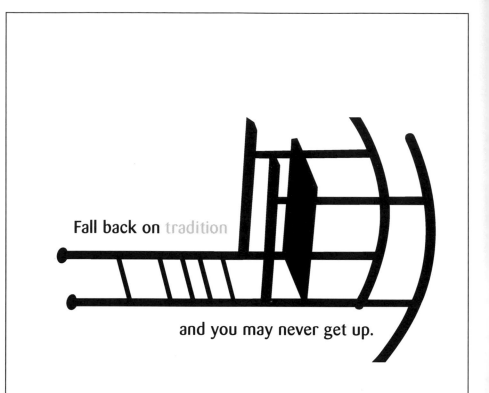

Fall back on tradition

and you may never get up.

Today's issues demand to be seen with a fresh
pair of eyes. Or 85,000 pairs with global vision
that can prepare you to be part of the future.
Not just part of history. Together, we can make
the future happen. Pull up a chair. www.eyuk.com

The functions of the non-executive director

Non-executive directors have a vital role to play in boardroom discussions. John Harper, IoD course leader and former IoD director of professional development, assesses their contribution

The 1992 Cadbury Report[1] initiated a debate about the main functions and responsibilities of non-executive directors. Today, it is widely accepted that independent non-executive directors have an important contribution to make to the proper running of companies and, therefore, more widely to the economy at large. As the Cadbury Report said, they: "should bring an independent judgment to bear on issues of strategy, performance, resources – including key appointments and standards of conduct".

Legally speaking, there is no distinction between executive and non-executive directors. As a consequence, in the UK unitary board structure, non-executive directors have the same legal duties, responsibilities and potential liabilities as their executive counterparts. Obviously, non-executive directors cannot give the same continuous attention to the business of the company.

However, it is important that they show the same commitment to its success as their executive colleagues.

All directors should be capable of seeing company and business issues in a broad perspective. Nonetheless, non-executive directors are usually chosen because they have a breadth of experience, are of relatively high calibre and have particular personal qualities. They may also have some specialist knowledge that will help provide the board with valuable insights or, perhaps, key contacts in related industries or the City. Of the utmost importance is their independence of the management of the company and any of its "interested parties". This means they can bring a degree of objectivity to the board's deliberations, playing a valuable role in its task of monitoring executive management.

The functions of non-executive directors

Essentially, the non-executive director role is to provide a creative contribution to the board by providing objective criticism. Non-executive directors are expected to focus on board matters and not stray into "executive direction", providing an independent view of the company that is removed from its day-to-day running. Non-executives directors, then, are appointed to bring to the board:

- independence;
- impartiality;
- wide experience;
- special knowledge;
- personal qualities.

Both the Cadbury and Hampel reports stress that the board should include independent non-executive directors of sufficient calibre and number for their views to carry significant weight in the board's decisions.

"Independent" directors, in this sense, are defined in the Cadbury Report as persons who "apart from directors' fees and shareholdings [are] independent of the management and free from any business or other relationships which could materially interfere with the exercise of the independent judgment".

The Stock Exchange's Combined Code advises that the balance of executive and non-executive directors should be such that no individual or small group of individuals can dominate the board's decision-taking. Non-executive directors should comprise not less than one-third of the board.

While much of the comment and discussion on non-executive directors tends to focus on listed companies, it is important to note that they can also make a valuable, albeit somewhat different, contribution to private companies. Indeed, there is a growing number of private companies, including relatively small ones, that is now actively searching for the "right" non-executive director.

Selection of non-executive directors

In view of the fact that non-executive directors have such a distinct role in ensuring the effectiveness of the board, it is perhaps important that they are selected with a greater degree of impartiality and care than the executive directors and senior management.

As with executive appointments, all board members should be involved in the decision to appoint them. When changes to board membership are necessary, the board should first assess the qualities and competencies already around the boardroom table, then develop specifications of the skills, personal qualities, knowledge and experience required for each new appointment and, after that, identify potential candidates. Non-executive appointments are no exception.

Non-executive directors should be chosen with regard to the balance of skills and experience on the board. They should be capable of providing an independent and impartial view of the board's considerations and decisions while also identifying strongly with the company's affairs.

It is thus essential to look for strength of character and the ability to stand back from the issue being discussed. Pragmatism and an ability to compromise are also vital. The demands of the role call for courage, integrity, common sense, good judgment, tenacity, diplomacy and an ability to listen carefully and to communicate with clarity, objectivity and brevity.

The specific background, experience and special disciplines required of the non-executive director will naturally depend on the qualities of the other directors on the board and the particular company concerned. Board-level experience of larger – but not necessarily related – enterprises is often needed. Business acumen and the kind of mind that focuses clearly on the matters in hand are essential.

Numeracy and the ability to gain an adequate understanding of the company's finances, its management, its employees, its special capabilities and its markets should also be ascertained when selecting a non-executive director.

The non-executive director's key responsibilities

Many chairmen use their non-executive directors to provide general counsel – and a different perspective – on matters of concern. They also seek their guidance on particular issues – before they are raised at board meetings. Indeed, some of the main specialist roles of a non-executive director will be carried out in a board sub-committee, especially in listed companies. The board's ability to operate efficiently is often increased by the establishment of sub-committees to give more detailed and objective consideration to major issues before they are formally discussed at the board. While the number of sub-committees varies from company to company, the key responsibilities of non-executive directors are constant. They lie in:

▶ Strategic direction

As an "outsider", the non-executive director should have a clearer or wider view of external factors affecting the company and its business environment than the executive directors. The normal role of the non-executive director in strategy formation is therefore to provide a creative and informed contribution and to act as a constructive critic in looking at the objectives and plans devised by the chief executive and his or her executive team.

▶ Troubleshooting

In times of crisis, occasions can arise when only the non-executive director is capable of acting on behalf of the company. This is especially true if a business has been badly managed and the chief executive or managing director needs to be replaced. It would be very difficult for the executive directors to take a lead at board level in these circumstances; non-executive directors have to take the initiative for them.

▶ Communication

The company's and board's effectiveness can benefit from outside contacts and opinions. An important function for non-executive directors, therefore, can be to help connect the business and board with networks of potentially useful people and organisations. In some cases, the non-executive director will be called upon to represent the company externally. The role of non-executive directors in corporate governance is discussed more fully by the Rt Hon John MacGregor in chapter 9. Broadly, however, duties to shareholders relate to:

▶ Audit

It is the duty of the whole board to ensure that the company accounts properly to its shareholders by presenting a true and fair reflection of its actions and financial performance and that the necessary internal control systems are put into place and monitored regularly and rigorously. A non-executive director has an important part to play in fulfilling this responsibility, whether or not a formal audit committee (composed of non-executive directors) of the board has been constituted.

▶ Remuneration of executive directors

Devising the appropriate remuneration packages for the executive directors can be one of the most contentious issues a board faces – not least because of the publicity executive pay has attracted in recent years. It is vital that decisions on executive remuneration, benefits and bonuses are seen to be made by those who do not stand to benefit directly from them. In listed companies and some larger private companies, therefore, policy on executive remuneration is usually decided by a committee of non-executive directors.

▶ Appointing directors

One of the board's most crucial functions is to decide on new appointments to the board and to other senior positions in the company. Again, in some cases, this is done within a committee, composed of executive and non-executive directors, whose task it is to ensure that appointments are made according to agreed specifications. Where implemented, the appraisal of directors is often tied directly into the selection and nomination process.

Opting for a non-executive director

The exact role and contribution of non-executive directors can appear hard to define. In large part, this stems from the myriad reasons for a board of directors choosing to appoint one. In addition, existing directors may have different expectations of the role from shareholders and other interested parties.

Common to many boards of directors and shareholders, however, is a growing acceptance that non-executive directors have a valued and necessary role to play in maximising board effectiveness. The introduction of truly independent judgment to the board's activities provides all interested parties with greater assurance that the correct strategies and decisions are likely to be chosen.

The contribution of non-executive directors can usually raise the level of discussion and improve the quality of decision-making on the board. This increases the chances of the company acting in the best interests of its long-term security and prosperity.

1. *Report of the Committee on the Financial Aspects of Corporate Governance*

Role at the SME

Lack of experience at the top can slow down the growth of young companies. Stocks Austin Sice, a fast-growing design company, solved the problem by appointing a non-executive chairman. Founding director David Stocks explains how

Stocks Austin Sice is a brand and communications consultancy advising a range of blue-chip clients – including Railtrack, BT and Burmah Castrol – on corporate identity and the use of print and new media. It has been established for 10 years and took on its first non-executive director after seven years.

February 11, 1995 was both an exciting and sad day for our company. It was the day we moved into new offices – the culmination of six years' hard work and a mark of our success and progress. But it was also the day that the father of one my partners died unexpectedly.

Robert had been a source of advice since the day we started the company, giving us both a blend of seasoned experience and objective common sense. Because he knew us so well he would never hold back from telling us when he considered us to be making a mistake – which was often!

About a year after this sad event we realised that our lack of that experience was holding us back and it was suggested that we think about employing a non-executive director. At first we resisted. Could we afford it? What would it add to our business? How would we find someone – and if we did and they were good, would they really want to work with us? It is easy to find excuses if you are not sure about an idea. After long debate, however, it was decided that we needed proper business guidance if we were to make further progress.

If I think now about the way topics were discussed and decisions were made in the days before the arrival of our non-executive director it makes me smile. There were no proper board meetings, only crisis meetings. We had no proper agendas and no-one acted as chairman. Difficult problems were ignored, while we concentrated on making the easy decisions. Polarised views were common; true reconciliations rare.

Using a search consultant

We were advised to use the IoD as a search consultant. This gave us two options. The first was a low-cost search from the IoD's databases.

However, the second option – which we chose – involved a more extensive service that included first-stage interviewing and the compilation of a shortlist. This cost us around £12,000 but was worth it for two reasons. First, it meant that a third party made the initial introduction for us. This is important as you are selling the company, not interviewing an employee; we have this tendency to be a little tough on ourselves, but our representative from the IoD was able to see all our good points. Secondly, time is always a precious commodity; having someone else prepare the ground meant we could get on with other things.

The brief emphasised the need to find someone who would understand the way our industry works and the shortlist did not disappoint. The six candidates included the head of a large publishing company famous for its support of design and the head of a very progressive property company developing warehouse apartments. Before we started the process of second interviews, another candidate was suggested by a photographer whom we often employed. Rather than approach this person direct, we passed his name to the IoD; they made contact and, after a meeting, recommended that he be added to the shortlist.

The interview experience

It was obvious that all the people we met had the skills we needed since they were all successful in their own right. Finding someone we felt we could work with was tougher. One was too bullish, one was not that interested and one was too busy, but I must say it was interesting to meet all the people we interviewed. We shortlisted two candidates and met them again over dinner to discuss their views on the company.

I would advise anyone who is going through this process to prepare questions carefully and to create an even playing field. I would even go so far as to meet in the same restaurant, as the atmosphere can make a difference. In our case, we supplied each of the candidates with the same set of questions in advance of the meetings. I would recommend due diligence to anyone looking for their first non-executive director. Having made a choice, we did take up references.

The process took about four months from briefing to appointment and in the end we chose our photographer's recommendation, David Lyon. To this you might say: "Why did we need the help of a professional organisation?" I have no regrets about the method we chose. The costs were not prohibitive and we received a lot of guidance for our money. I also think that as a small company we would not have been taken so seriously if we'd made the initial approaches ourselves.

The choice

David had been the chief executive of Rexam, the paper, print and packaging company. His business knowledge is first rate and he demonstrated an interest in design during our meetings. Having started out trying to find someone who understood design issues, we ended up choosing David for his business knowledge. We decided that he should act as chairman as my co-founders and I held an equal shareholding in the company.

Having a non-executive director costs us about £2,000 per day (for 12-15 days a year), but it is obvious that David is not "in it for the money". He could do much better financially than work with us; the fact that we are a different kind of business makes the position interesting.

The contribution you need a non-executive director to make to your business will depend largely on the type of sector you are in. We work in a service industry and our deadlines are often tight. We employ about 30 people, which makes us a medium-sized design company, and our earnings potential is high as the majority of employees are graduate-level educated. This means that our margins are not like those in a manufacturing business. There is little income stream and we rely on the standard of our portfolio to generate the next project with forward fees changing daily. Finally, designers are notoriously difficult to manage. As the joke goes: "How many designers does it take to change a light bulb? The designers' reply is: 'Does it have to be a light bulb?'" We are always trying to balance the process-driven elements to what we do with the creative and often necessarily undisciplined elements that are crucial to our success.

The chairman's contributions

One of the first recommendations that David made was that we held quarterly board meetings away from our office with a set agenda and no interruptions from staff. This is one simple example of the discipline that having a non-executive chairman has brought to our business. On David's recommendation, we have appointed a full-time accountant to act as head of finance. This means we are up to speed with current accounting practices, and monthly management accounts are prepared to a consistent standard in shorter timescales. We consult David on remuner-ation policy and investment in capital expenditure.

One of David's most important contributions was made in the past few months when one of our founders decided to leave to pursue new ideas. As anyone who has been in this situation will know, this can be a traumatic time, resulting in the loss of long-term friendships. We were determined that this would not happen in our case and agreed that our chairman, who has no equity interest in the business, would act as a totally impartial judge on the valuation of the company. In this matter, David has proved invaluable, providing non-emotive advice on a number of very important issues. We remain the best of friends with our former partner and believe that the agreement that was reached was fair to both parties.

Another important, but unexpected, contribution that David has made is directly business related. We are often talking to the senior members of FTSE companies and it is often useful to get the opinion of someone who has been a chief executive of a large public company. It may not change your opinion, but it might affect how you present your case.

The skills that our chairman brings are complementary to ours. It would be easy to try to look for someone who is a senior member of the industry that you are working in, but in the field of internet work, where we are very active, those people do not exist. We have no shortage of ideas, but a shortage of experience.

Finally, and perhaps most importantly, the personality fit is vital. Can I work with this person? David understands the style of the company well and makes his contribution in a very convincing manner that does not ruffle feathers.

We were told that a non-executive director could have a limited lifespan for our business – after which we might not be able to keep learning and would need to recruit a new non-executive director. I don't know if this is true, but I can see our present chairman continuing for the foreseeable future and would recommend any young and growing business to consider the value of a non-executive director.

Becoming a non-executive director in an SME

Allen L. Thomas, a non-executive chairman of a number of SME companies, advises not leaving independent directorships until retirement age. They have much to teach those in mid-career

Many businessmen and women think about becoming non-executive directors in one or more companies at some point in their careers.

In my case, the decision evolved over a period of time. Having moved to London after retiring as a partner in a New York-based international law firm, I found I had some time on my hands. My first non-executive directorship came on the recommendation of a friend. He had been asked to take the appointment himself, but had identified a conflict of interest. This was the start – not a planned or particularly well-thought-through start – but a start.

I'm glad I made it. For those of us who believe that life is about learning, a non-executive directorship is a new opportunity to stay active and learn.

The prospect of the end of one's career, of suddenly not having to get up and go to work, of not interacting with others, of not accomplishing a job of work, can be terrifying for the busy executive. As a non-executive director, one learns a new or different business, meets new and different people, confronts new and different problems, is engaged, busy, valued.

For a rising or risen executive not currently contemplating retirement, the non-executive appointment is a new challenge that can expand the database and broaden the horizons.

The commitment

It follows that a non-executive role is not a commitment to undertake lightly – whatever your age. The benefits are great but so are the demands. A directorship, whether executive or non-executive, carries very real legal and moral responsibilities. Anyone who is still in a job, or is relishing a leisurely retirement after a long, stressful business career should ask themselves whether they are willing to take on another demand on their precious time – whether they really can face dealing with any more tension.

The vicissitudes of business life mean that you will not always have control over the amount of time you need to spend on non-executive work. Just what the commitment entails is something to think carefully about before accepting an appointment. Bear in mind that if you have retired you will probably not have the support staff to help you to cope with the paperwork and other administrative tasks.

It would be a mistake to generalise about the amount of work involved. I now devote at least half my time to non-executive directorships but, to be sure, some of the pressure on me derives from being chairman of two public companies. A non-executive chairmanship requires much more work than a non-executive directorship in the same company.

In my experience, SMEs require more time in proportion to their size than larger companies. They have, or feel able to afford, fewer outside resources, such as financial advisers, management consultants and lawyers, and their management usually have less experience outside the field of their own operations. In such cases, non-executive directors sometimes have to support management in ways that might otherwise be handled – for a price – by outsiders.

So far, I have not had to give up any directorship because of demands on my time, but I have declined to take on new ones. I have had to hire a part-time secretary to cope with the paperwork. I recharge her cost to my directorships *pro-rata*.

Looking for an appointment

If you do decide that the pressures are a price worth paying, should you look for a post in your own sector or outside it? My first non-executive directorship was with a large Lloyd's managing agency, embroiled, as all were at the time, in the Lloyd's problems. Insurance was a field I had worked in as a lawyer, so it was not entirely new – which helped in getting the offer.

While the familiar is often comforting, the different can be more rewarding. Subsequent directorships have led me further afield. My work in the high-tech sector, for example, is newer to me and has presented a real learning experience.

So, how do you go about getting a non-executive directorship? In my experience, you are likely to be confronted with two difficulties. First, is a supply and demand problem: it is clear that more people want positions - for the right or the wrong reasons – than there are positions available. Second, in a classic "Catch 22" situation, you cannot get a directorship unless you have a directorship.

It is important, particularly if you are seeking your first non-executive directorship, to get the timing right. Starting when you retire, or are preparing for retirement, is likely to be a mistake. Increasingly, boards are looking for non-executive talent outside the pool of retired or retiring friends of the chairman or the chief executive: the Stock Exchange's Combined Code encourages such behaviour. Begin in mid-career, when energy, current experience and current contacts make you much more attractive.

There are at least four good places to start looking for non-executive directorships: specialist headhunters; generalist head-hunters; venture capitalists; advisers (accountants, lawyers, etc.). Don't, however, shun the old-boy network completely – it works more often than it is fashionable to admit. The old boy network helped me find my first appointment. The IoD's headhunting service and a venture capitalist put me on to others.

The interview

Of course, the first contact with the company isn't everything. You will have to sell yourself. However grand you are, or have been in your former working life, do not be too proud to be interviewed – and to perform well.

All the old, or never learned, skills of job search apply. Do your homework; know your target. Get as much information about what they are looking for before you tell them what you are offering – and make your adjustments appropriately.

The decision-makers will almost certainly be much younger than you, so pay attention to your energy and enthusiasm level. Listen as well as talk; display your depth of knowledge, but also show a willingness to learn. Once you have your first directorship, others seem to be easier to find.

When things go wrong

As I have tried to make clear, a non-executive role is no sinecure. If all is going well and you think that you have a rather good deal as a non-executive of a UK listed company, start worrying: it can only be a matter of time before the tough questions land in your lap. Is the chief executive, or another key member of the executive team, past his sell-by date? Has proper succession planning been made? Have the entrepreneur's optimism and enthusiasm blinded the company to the reality of market conditions and destroyed his or her credibility among analysts? Is the new plant or corporate acquisition that is being urged by the advisers and managers going to be be in shareholders' interests or merely in the interest of executives' egos and the advisors' bank balances? Is a profits warning required? Do the advisers need changing? Are proposed related party transactions properly considered and authorised? Are the venture capitalists' expectations going to be met? Do the accounts properly reflect both generally accepted accounting policy and reality?

The list is infinite. When things go wrong, or do not go as planned, non-executives really earn their money. Advisers can advise, but directors – executive and non-executive – must decide and take responsibility.

In these situations, what do the non-executives do? You cannot play the "gotcha" brand of directorship, where you lie in wait for a director to make a mistake. First, you should adhere to good process; get proper outside advice where appropriate; debate and consider; apply your own knowledge and experience to add to, and be a filter for, that of the executive directors and advisers. You should also call meetings and ask questions. Do not shrink from saying "no" or try to "get along, by going along". In summary, you need clear judgment and personal integrity if you are going to discharge your responsibility to the shareholders of the company.

Usually, good process, personal integrity and the expenditure of energy will resolve the issues at hand. If they do not, then the non-executive directors should – with proper advice – withdraw their support of the company and resign. I do not mean to overdramatise; I have experienced no such non-executive exits personally. But directorships are not for the faint hearted. Some may call them challenging; others may call them scary.

For me, life is about learning and adventure; being a non-executive director keeps you in the game.

View from the top

Today, independent directors of public companies have more responsibilities than ever before. Do they also get more satisfaction from their roles? The Rt. Hon. John MacGregor OBE PC MP recounts his own experiences

All the different roles of a non-executive director – regulatory policeman, ethical watchdog, shareholder representative and practical adviser – are important on a plc board. However, with their wider experience, non-executive directors have an important role to play not just as advisers to their boards but also as active participants in the strategy of the business and in ensuring that the executive directors are carrying out the board policy in an effective manner.

I find that some of the most rewarding work I do with companies is in strategic discussions as well as in working policy issues. Offering a wider perspective on strategic issues and giving experienced judgment on the papers presented by the executive directors is one of the most rewarding functions of a non-executive. Strategic awaydays are a crucial part of one's work.

Serving on a plc board means dealing with all the compliance issues, the Stock Exchange Code and all the matters arising from the Cadbury, Greenbury and Hampel Committees. I have heard it said that the increased responsibilities of non-executives in these areas are putting some people off, but I've had no experience of that myself.

It is certainly true that the legal responsibilities and the workload of the non-executive have both grown, but I welcome that and I haven't heard anyone complaining about it. People who have spent a long time in one company or industry and have reached the level of finance director, chief executive or chairman, find it helpful to their career paths – and probably to their own businesses – to broaden their experience by becoming a non-executive in other industries.

Time commitment

Just what is involved? For each company, there is normally one board meeting a month. In merger or takeover situations, however, there can be a considerable number of emergency meetings, and you have to make sure that you are either there or plugged in – in one way or another – to what is going on. Audit and remuneration committee meetings are additional and there will be extra meetings, lunches, dinners and telephone calls when critical issues are around.

Then there is the time spent in preparation for board meetings. This will vary with the company, but one that is very active in its strategy can involve its non-executive directors in a substantial amount of paperwork. Some companies, for example, will put every proposition that involves expenditure above a certain figure to the board for approval.

I also try to get round as much of the company as I can to familiarise myself on the ground – which I was always doing as a minister. I believe that it's important for people to see that you are there so that they have a chance to talk to you about issues and perhaps let off steam.

The total time commitment can vary between 15 and 24 days a year if you add in all the bits and pieces.

Accepting an appointment

The search for non-executives is becoming more professional. My impression is that companies are increasingly going to headhunters. On the other hand, if they know exactly what they are looking for – perhaps someone to add strength to the finance director in a multinational business – they may ask their merchant banking advisers for recommendations. It is important that the nominations committee or the board or whoever is choosing the non-executives should be very clear about the kind of background and skills they are looking for to complement the other independent directors.

Equally, non-executives need to brief themselves on the issues facing the particular business and its industry. Even where I knew quite a lot about the sectors – for example, the food industry through my work as minister for agriculture, fisheries and food, and the financial services business through my experience at the Treasury – I had quite long conversations with the chairman and chief executive before I accepted the appointment. In one or two cases, the headhunters made available to me on a strictly confidential basis all the papers from previous strategic awayday meetings indicating some of the key issues facing the company. Of course, before taking on an appointment one also looks very thoroughly at the report and accounts – going way back. And – what might seem at first a small, but nevertheless crucial, point – one needs to make sure that the board and committee dates fit one's diary!

The non-executive director's perspective

One can't always tell what part of one's experience is going to help with a company's specific problems. My experience as a minister has been useful with regard to the genetically modified foods issue; I can help with advice on how to handle food scares; how to avoid getting into difficult situations. In merger and takeover situations, I've been able to help assess whether it was a deal that could be put to shareholders and whether the conditions on which we were going in were right.

My experience of the Treasury and of economic matters in general has also enabled me to contribute. There are different personal views on the single currency on all the boards that I'm on, but I think my place as a non-executive director has been to ensure that companies are prepared on a practical basis to deal with the euro, whether the UK goes in or not, rather than to help form corporate policy on the issue.

Only occasionally have there been areas of conflict on the board that I have had to try to help resolve. The non-executive is, however, an independent person to whom the executives can come and chat – and to that extent he or she may be helpful in resolving crises or conflicts.

Nor have I ever found it difficult to get the information that I felt I needed. In every case, I've been impressed by the quality of the information that comes forward; where I have asked for more, it has always been made available. The language used in the reports that actuaries make to insurance companies has caused some difficulties. This, of course, is all tied up with regulatory requirements, but I hope that sometimes my comments have resulted in clearer reports the next time round.

A vital part of the non-executive director's role, while not in any way compromising his or her independence, is to secure good relationships with the board, and, of course, the key relationships are with the chairman and chief executive. In any role in life you may have to take unpleasant decisions but it is important to gain the confidence of one's colleagues. A non-executive's perspective has to be much broader than that of the executive directors, who sometimes tend to restrict their views and comments to their own specific areas of responsibility – unless the chairman encourages them to do otherwise.

Corporate governance

Although I was not a non-executive director in the pre-Cadbury era, one can see quite clearly three or four areas where the new guidelines have had an impact and where more time is now being spent. One is the audit committee, where you are signing up at the end of the day to certain commitments in the annual report.

Another is the remuneration committee, not simply because executive pay has received so much public attention and you have a clear responsibility to the shareholders to ensure that remuneration is balanced and proper, but also because it is very important to get the remuneration package right if you are to attract the right people and get the right motivation. All the corporate governance and compliance issues involve a discipline to ensure you are regularly giving attention to these things, but a huge amount that flows from it is what you should have been doing anyway.

Then there are external factors such as environmental issues, food scares, the euro and globalisation to consider. Since 1996 we have also all been spending a lot of time on the Year 2000 issue, ensuring that all the processes are there and have been followed through to minimise to the greatest possible extent any problems arising from the Millennium Bug.

One also has to be alert to media scrutiny and the way in which public opinion is increasingly shaping developments. However, I think it is disappointing that wider share owner-ship – in which I have always been a passionate believer – has not led to wider involvement by the ordinary shareholder in their companies.

One of the things I had to come up to speed on as a non-executive was the amount of attention and care given to the institutional shareholders. I would like to see the ordinary shareholder given the same treatment. The fact is, however, that the great mass of ordinary shareholders don't want to get involved in issues of strategy, investment or takeover; the institutional shareholders, on the other hand, do keep you on your toes.

John MacGregor has been Conservative MP for South Norfolk for 25 years. His career has been a mixture of business and politics. He was Chief Secretary to the Treasury 1985-87, Minister of Agriculture, Fisheries and Food 1987-89, Secretary of State for Education and Science 1989-90, Lord President of the Council and Leader of the House of Commons 1990-92 and Secretary of State for Transport 1992-94. He is currently a non-executive director of the food companies Unigate and ABF, of the mutual Friends Provident and of Slough Estates.

View from the institutional investor

Michelle Edkins, corporate governance executive of Hermes Investment Management, stresses that keeping watch on company communication policy is a vital part of the non-executive role

The Anglo-American corporate model of capitalism recognises maximising shareholder value as a key objective and shareholder supervision of management as a contributing factor to superior long-term returns. The onus is on the committed shareholders of the company to hold directors accountable, taking, if necessary, the ultimate sanction of voting poorly performing directors out of office. It follows, therefore, that the right to vote is an asset that should be managed with thought.

But to vote in a considered way shareholders need information. Without it, they will be unable to assess how well directors have met financial and strategic objectives and managed relationships with employees, suppliers, customers and other stakeholders. In response to the growing trend among shareholders to take an active role in the stewardship of the company, the more progressive companies have made improving communication with shareholders a priority.

Clearly, most communication between the company, its shareholders and others has to come from those people who have an intimate knowledge of the day-to-day running of the business – the executive directors.

Non-executive directors, however, do have a role to play in the company's communications with shareholders and others with a legitimate interest in the business. As the Hampel Committee reported in 1998, non-executive directors contribute in this area, as in others, through working co-operatively with their executive colleagues and exercising robust independence of judgment when necessary.

The role of the senior non-executive

The Hampel Committee recognised that there can be "occasions when there is a need to convey concerns to the board other than through the chairman or chief executive officer". After the chairman, the independent director most likely to be required to be involved in communication with shareholders, and possibly stakeholders, is the senior non-executive director.

As outlined in its corporate governance policy, Hermes sees the role of the senior non-executive director as an extension of that of deputy chairman, combining the roles of independent deputy chairman and senior non-executive director. We believe that the main responsibilities are to ensure that the views of each non-executive director are given due consideration and to provide a channel of communication between non-executive directors and shareholders. This communication channel should be in addition to – and not a replacement for – existing channels. For many companies, it may have only occasional use.

Although there has been much talk of the potential for divisiveness if this channel is opened, we would argue that, if the right person is appointed and the situation is handled with sensitivity, this should not be so.

Hermes takes advantage of the non-executive development programmes offered by Henley Management College, Spencer Stuart, Cranfield School of Management, the Non-Executive Directors' Forum and the IoD to address non-executive directors from a wide range of companies. Our aim is not only to explain our stance as a shareholder but also to learn what participants see as the significant issues affecting them.

The need for better information

The relationship between the company and its so-called stakeholders is a growing area of interest. One of the core difficulties for anyone wishing to assess the performance of directors on non-financial matters such as corporate governance, environmental impact and employee relations is the paucity of public information. The disclosure on these topics provided in the annual report is all too often formulaic and seldom insightful.

As the annual report is still the first thing many people turn to when gathering information on a company, it seems sensible to use it as a communication tool rather than merely as a disclosure document. It should be written so that the reader comes away better informed about the company, its achievements and its prospects. Unfortunately, too many annual reports still fail to achieve this aim. This is particularly true of the sections of the annual report presumably drafted by the non-executive directors, namely the chairman's statement and the remuneration report.

Directors' remuneration is, rightly or wrongly, the focus of many readers of annual reports. The Hampel Committee expected companies to provide a narrative statement of how in practice they apply the accepted corporate governance principles to their particular circumstances. However, many committees seem to draft their report from a template of platitudes such as "the company's share option scheme is designed to attract, retain and motivate key personnel".

Surely attracting, retaining and motivating is the *raison d'être* of all (good) incentive schemes? What shareholders and other users of the annual report want to know is how the scheme achieves this goal, what type of people the directors are trying to recruit, how the split between basic pay, annual bonus and long-term incentive pay reflects the focus of the board on performance and accountability, and so on. Providing such specific information does not necessarily mean a bulkier annual report. A few well-chosen words can convey a lot more than the clichés seen in poorer quality annual reports.

A key question non-executive directors should ask when the board reviews the effectiveness of the company's communication policy is whether there is other information that could be provided to shareholders. Is it relevant, for example, to provide details of fines incurred from – or relations with – UK and EU regulators such as the Health and Safety Executive, environmental agencies and the Stock Exchange? Perhaps more information on training policy, relations with trade unions, staff turnover and health and safety programmes would be helpful.

All of this information is usually readily available to the board (ie. it is information already being collected by management). It should be readily available to shareholders – on request or over the internet – if not in the annual report.

Such disclosures should reflect the relative significance of the issues to the company and include information about the risks associated with wrongly assessing their importance.

The risks of bad communication

Communication policy and its effective implementation must also be of interest to the non-executive directors. There are quantifiable risks to a company if its communication strategy does not work. Most commonly, the result of poor communication is a divergence in shareholder and management expectations that is eventually reflected in the share price.

All non-executive directors should take advantage of any opportunities that arise to visit company sites and to meet executives and staff outside head office.

It may also be worth newly appointed non-executive directors (and on occasion, the more seasoned non-executives) joining the executives on a round of results meetings in the City so that they can hear firsthand of issues that concern shareholders and that could, potentially, affect the share price. Shareholders can, in turn, assess for themselves the calibre of the non-executives.

Non-executives at the AGM

All the activities mentioned thus far are, in large part, undertaken in private. The most public role that the non-executives are likely to take in the communication of company policy, performance and prospects is at the annual general meeting. As stated in the Combined Code: "The chairman of the board should arrange for the chairman of the audit, remuneration and nomination committees to be available to answer questions at the AGM."

In many companies, this means that all the non-executive directors should attend the annual general meeting. Of course, the AGM is widely criticised as ineffective and many expect some major reforms in the next few years. But the insight to be gained from meeting with private shareholders, some of whom may be employees or other stakeholders, can make the AGM a worthwhile – if perhaps daunting – experience.

In conclusion, if shareholders are to exercise stewardship of companies they need detailed information on the performance of the directors in discharging their diverse responsibilities. Non-executive directors have an important contribution to make in ensuring the relevant information is communicated to share-holders. And despite their being generally out of the limelight, their role in influencing the company's approach to communication with shareholders and stakeholders can have a significant impact on the fortunes of the company.

Michelle Edkins communicates Hermes' voting policies and decisions direct to companies. She is also involved in policy development and research into companies where there is potential to unlock value through shareholder activism.

Hermes is the executive arm of the BT Pension Scheme (BTPS). In recognition of its responsibilities on behalf of clients to participate in the stewardship of companies, it has a Statement on Corporate Governance and Voting Policy. The Trustees of the BTPS and Post Office pension schemes have delegated responsibility to Hermes to vote on their behalf in accordance with the policy. As a result, Hermes votes proxies at over 1,200 general and extraordinary company meetings in the UK each year.

The future of the independent director

The changes reshaping business life have profound implications for the role of the independent director. Nigel Macdonald, senior partner at Ernst & Young, charts a move from supporting cast to centre stage

It is axiomatic that business life is accelerating in pace and increasing in complexity. A genuine shift is taking place in the way we do business.

The process is characterised on a number of levels. One of the most relevant, for the independent director, is the emergence of laterally diversified companies: those that have branched out into areas that add value to their core business. Supermarket chains, for example, now offer internet service provision, insurance and financial services, affinity/loyalty cards and other services along with their traditional activity of selling food and household supplies.

This process of divergence is radically different from the traditional, upstream-downstream vertical diversification, where the synergy between the different parts of the company was reasonably evident.

It differs also from that of the conglomerate, where obvious connectivity between the parts of the corporation was neither looked for nor expected. The activities that link the laterally diversified company may be limited to shared management, common financial and administrative systems and common branding.

Monitoring strategic alliances

Another characteristic of the changing business world is a very high reliance on outsourcing or strategic alliances with other companies. Call-centre arrangements, internet facilities, financial packages and added-value customer services often need to be co-developed. Thus, collaborating with the laterally diversified supermarket may be a bank, a healthcare insurance firm and a travel agent – all of whom may be household names in their own right.

This kind of collaboration has startling implications. It means that, for both corporate buyer and corporate supplier, failure in a wholly unrelated industry may, through a process of linkages probably invisible to the consumer, have a hugely detrimental effect on the balance sheet. For the outsourcer, it also means that the maintenance of brand values could largely be in the hands of independent suppliers, which may or may not prove reliable in the long term.

Monitoring the effectiveness of the tie-ins and strategic alliances that will inform the connected, yet highly diversified, commercial landscape of the future will therefore be a key role for independent directors. Indeed, independent directors are, almost by definition, ideally placed for this task. Potentially, they bring networking skills and experiences of other industries and other methodologies that will be invaluable to companies seeking new ways of delivering goods and services. Their ability to challenge the assumptions made by their executive colleagues and to identify and address risks will be a really valuable service to the shareholder.

Risk manager and watchman

The 1999 Turnbull report argued that business risk management is an explicit responsibility of the non-executive director. Since there are many risks attached to third-party relationships, the work of the independent members of the board can, therefore, only increase: questions relating to intellectual property, the ownership and protection of data, service design and exit strategies from unsuccessful or outdated relationships are all going to tax the non-executive director.

The changing nature of business also calls on the independent director to exercise to the full his or her skills as constructive challenger. He or she needs to question perceived norms.

In any particular business, sector or industry, there may be some elements that have not changed from year to year. It may be the market structure. It may be the process. It may be physical or structural constraints. Eventually, these features become so much part of the landscape to the individual company or industry that they are seen as immutable. But they are not. They are merely assumptions that have not changed for some time.

The trick to winning in business is to keep alert to "givens" that are not givens at all – and to understand what is going to affect them, be it new technology, new trading practice, liberalisation either domestically or internationally, or changes in consumer aspirations and needs. The independent director has to help keep watch, to see the wood for the trees.

Thinking the unthinkable

The value of challenging historical assumptions is becoming more obvious. In today's fast-changing world, little can be taken for granted. Nothing demonstrates this more clearly than the UK energy industry. Several years ago, few people would have predicted that gas companies would one day supply household electricity – not least because of all the regulatory obstacles that such a crossover then faced. Even fewer would have predicted that a gas company would diversify outside the energy sector. Today, the concept of a combined utilities company is taken almost as read. And Centrica is merging with the AA.

The Centrica deal neatly underscores the change in how we view connectivity between industries. Although it met with some hostile reaction, it is a perfectly logical extension of the lateral model. Centrica sees itself not as a gas company, but as a manager of information, using call-centre technology as a platform to sell other products.

Good independent directors are particularly well-placed, being one step back from day-to-day management, to watch out for and identify the issues that could change a company. They need to think the unthinkable. Often the things that could happen do happen. Today, to say that the internet is changing the way businesses and individual consumers make purchases is to state the obvious. But only five years ago its impact was far from evident. A travel agency, say, would then have assumed that high-street shops and advertising would continue to be its typical outlet to customers – this had been the case for so long that it was assumed to be permanent.

None of this is to suggest that the independent director needs to be an expert at crystal-ball gazing. In fulfilling their role, independent directors will be aided by the capture and exploitation of data, particularly, of course, that of customer demographics. But within the corporation, somebody needs to have the independence of mind, and the depth of experience, to start seeing how new developments might change the businesses in which they operate.

The really slick company is the one that is capable of totally repositioning itself to respond to changing business needs. Who would now believe, for example, that mobile phone company Nokia used to be a major paper manufacturer? Nokia is still in the communications business, of course, it is just that the delivery mechanism – cellular telephony rather than ink on paper – has changed.

In all this we need to recognise that it is individual people that are important. The technology that powers the internet may well be impressive, but the impetus to use it as a worldwide communications tool came from individuals – not governments or regulatory bodies.

Innovators, first in academia then in the broader community, saw the wider potential of an information exchange system that was originally designed to protect US military communications in time of nuclear war. Business has been running to catch up ever since. For many industries the question "yes, the internet is impressive – but how do I make money out of it?" remains at best only partially answered.

It is not just new technology that needs watching. The technology that drives rapid change may not be new. It may be well established, so well established that it is taken for granted – until it is suddenly used in new and innovative ways. First Direct and Direct Line, for example, have had a dramatic impact on the banking and insurance sectors by their use of an old technology – the telephone.

The new professionalism

The businesses that succeed in the future will surely be those that harness the talents of visionaries and entrepreneurs in a multi-faceted, multi-skilled environment that involves cross-industry partnerships. They will be those that are aware of the emergence of corporate governance – the way we manage companies – as a world theme in business thinking. Despite differences in emphasis and interpretation in the various major economies, the whole of the western world now recognises that if companies are the engine of the local economy, excellence in corporate governance is of real importance to each nation. Both these trends will continue to work towards placing the independent director at centre stage.

The role of independent director of the future will be greatly enhanced. Making sure there is a generation of men and women ready for it will be a vital challenge. The development of the emerging profession of independent director will be inextricably linked to the development of good businesses and of strong economies.

The Combined Code and the non-executive director's role

The Code of Best Practice incorporated in the Combined Code includes several specific references to non-executive directors:

▶ The board should include non-executive directors of sufficient calibre and number for their views to carry significant weight in the board's decisions. Non-executive directors should comprise not less than one third of the board.

▶ The majority of non-executive directors should be independent of management and free from any business or other relationship which could materially interfere with the exercise of their independent judgement. Non-executive directors considered by the board to be independent in this sense should be identified in the annual report.

▶ A majority of the members of a nomination committee should be non-executive directors and the chairman should be either the chairman of the board or a non-executive director.

▶ Remuneration committees should consist exclusively of non-executive directors.

▶ An audit committee should also consist exclusively of non-executive directors, a majority of whom should be independent non-executive directors.

▶ Non-executive directors should be appointed for specified terms and re-appointment should not be automatic.